WHOSE ARE YOU REALLY, JERUSALEM?

Facts you should know in the struggle for the future of Jerusalem

By

Kobi Shashoua

From the book series

"Understanding the Middle East"

WHOSE ARE YOU REALLY, JERUSALEM?

Jerusalem – is it the eternal capital of the Jewish people?

Tel: +97254-8030648

Email Address: kobimnsil@gmail.com

Website: www.kobisha.com

Clarification

Every few years Israel is awakened to a brutal bloodbath provoked by the slogan "Al Aqsa is in danger". The latest wave started in October 2015 when this slogan was delivered proudly by clergymen, opinion leaders among the Palestinians and the Arabs living in Israel. This call out was enough to excite many Palestinians and Arabs in Israel to launch an indiscriminate campaign of stabbing and terror among the "Jews". In fact, this call out is unfounded since the status quo regarding the administration of the holy sites in Jerusalem has been uninterrupted for decades, but the facts, in fact, are of no consequence. The wave of terror when every day Jews are stabbed by ecstatic terrorists has become a daily reality in Israel. The religious pretext actually raises the question regarding the status of Jerusalem among religions. Is Jerusalem indeed a religious and national center of the Palestinian people or does it belong to the Jewish people from time immemorial? In this book we shall examine this issue thoroughly and leave the reader to draw the conclusions.

ABOUT THE AUTHOR

Kobi Shashoua is an author and a lecturer. Among his books you can find the most comprehensive book that exists to date bout the Israeli-Palestinian conflict "Israel: the truth, the whole truth and nothing but the truth." This book leads the reader chapter by chapter through the complex reality of the conflict and dissects the causes for the crisis, uncovers to the reader the true faces of the parties involved, and presents the tactics, the strategies and the true objectives, that lie below the surface. The author also wrote the book series: "Facts you should know about the Middle East".The book you are holding in your hands is from that series.

The author, who resides in Israel, which is located in the most dangerous neighborhood of the world, in the heart of the Middle East, shares with us the facts together with the insights and the unique understanding of the region where he lives. We invite you to take part in this journey from a safe distance.

TABLE OF CONTENTS:

Foreword

Jerusalem, the holly city for the tree religions: Judaism, Christianity and Islam, is currently governed by Israel. Where does the sanctity of Jerusalem come from? Why is Jerusalem so important to Jews, to Christians and to Muslims? Why is the establishment of a Palestinian state conditional to Jerusalem being its capital? How can the same city be the capital of two countries?

Another stage in the war of the Arabs, while the Palestinians are used as the spearhead, is the severance of the ties between the Jewish people and their homeland and by turning them into "imperialistic conquerors". Severance of the moral bond, blurs the legacy that Abraham the forefather has left to his children and to the People of Israel and truth is replaced by lies.

The Jewish people are connected with firm bonds to their historical land. The Palestinians know that very well, and spread malicious propaganda all over the world that descends upon attentive ears.

The ancestors of the Jewish people are buried all over the country. Rachel's Tomb, Joseph's Tomb, the Cave of the Patriarchs – are today in "Palestinian" territories that are named "the occupied territories".

Rewriting history - an example for severing the ties between the Jewish people   and their historic homeland.

I shall refer briefly to the site of Rachel's Tomb and demonstrate how propaganda can create a reality, a reality in cooperation with the UN.

Rachel was one of the four mothers of the People of Israel. Jacob married her and she gave birth to Joseph and Benjamin. Her story is told in genesis, chapter C"T – L"H (1). A tradition from the late Second Temple period considers her place of burial at the northern entrance of Bethlehem, south of Jerusalem.

The tomb is a place of worship for the Jews, and it consists of two chapels – one for men and one for women. Tens of thousands of people visit the place on the eleventh day of Heshvan that is accepted today as the day Rachel died, to pray at her grave.

Not only the Jews refer to the place as Rachel's Tomb. The Muslims call it that too.

The Muslims have been referring to the place as Rachel's Tomb for the last few hundred years, and they call it "Kubat Rachel". Until recent years the place has been called "Kubat Rachel" in Palestinian publications, as well, for example: in the Palestinian lexicon published by the Arab League and the PLO in 1984, and in another lexicon published in 1996. In the book "Palestine – the Holy Land" it is written: "At the northern entrance to the city is Rachel's Tomb, the mother of all mothers, who died while giving birth to Benjamin". Thus also in the book "The West Bank and Gaza – Palestine" the place is mentioned as Rachel`s Tomb.

There is no doubt about the sanctity of the place for the Jewish people whose one of their earliest mothers is buried there. This fact did not go unnoticed by the Muslims as well, who have called it for hundreds of years by the same name.

During the Ottoman occupation non-Muslims were forbidden to enter the site. Mohammad, Governor of Jerusalem, renovated the site and gave the Jews exclusivity over it.

---

(1) From Wikipedia under "Rachel"

A drawing of Rachel's Tomb, 1585, from the book by the Christian tourist Zolrat. (2)

In modern times, things went wrong. The Tomb is no longer a tomb, and the entire area is an "occupied area". As of the end of 2015 the tomb is an enclave within the territories of the Palestinian Authority. Hence, in order to get to pray at a sacred place for the Jews, visitors risk their lives.

Therefore, in September 2002 the Israeli government decided that the site of the Tomb   will belong to the Israeli side of the security fence, and the route to the site was fortified   with concrete walls and with observation posts. In 2003 the Institute of Rachel's Tomb was founded. The Institute provides armored busses that drive Jewish worshipers to the Tomb site.

The Palestinian Minister of Religious Affairs defined the Tomb site as a mosque [3]. If so, who has been actually lying in this ancient grave, thousands of years before Islam was founded?

How, nevertheless, to solve such a contradiction? Quite simply: changing the designation of the place. It is no longer a tomb but a mosque

---

(2) The picture is from Wikipedia under "Rachel"

(3) From Wikipedia under "Rachel's Tomb"

In February 2010, Mr. Benjamin Netanyahu, the Prime Minister of Israel, declared that the Tomb will be a National Heritage Site. It is logical for the Israeli government to wish to renovate and restore the area of the sacred Tomb. But remember, logic is not a steady matter, as a wise Jew said recently:

"Only two things are infinite, the universe and human stupidity, and I'm not sure about the former". [4]

The intention of the Israeli government to restore one of the sacred places for the Jews   triggered a wave of protest from the UN, from Palestinian officials, from Arab governments and from the United States. Most outspoken was the Prime Minster of Turkey, Erdogan, who said: "The tomb has never been and will never be a sacred   place for the Jews and that is because it is a Muslim site."

As is well known, when it comes to Israel the UN knows how to allocate huge resources in order to condemn it. Not long afterwards, in response to the declaration by the Israeli Prime Minister, the Executive Board of UNESCO [5] declared that the structure is located in Palestinian territories, and any action by Israel in the area will constitute a violation of international law and the relevant treaties.

"Violation" of international law was performed because the Israeli government declared an area sacred to the Jews in a region defined as an occupied Palestinian territory. If so, what is a tomb that is considered the second most important site for Jews doing there?

The Israeli ambassador made his comments during a meeting of the Board, and the resolution of UNESCO was to declare Rachel's Tomb as the Bilal Aben Raba mosque. Since the comments by the Israeli ambassador are justified, they should be deleted. And if all this is not enough, notice how the lie turns into the truth. How Rachel's Tomb turns into a mosque, and hence it is no longer necessary to explain who is buried in the site. So, everyone will know that there has always been here a Muslim mosque, and the Jews are just hallucinating that this is a sacred place for them. Ask "UNESCO", they even declare that. Thus, the Palestinians do not only succeed to slowly disintegrate the bond between the Jewish people and their homeland, they receive a "stamp of approval" from the UN, that ignores history and declares one of the sacred places for the Jews as a mosque, and contributes this way to the severance of a historical bond that made the UN vote in 1947 for the establishment of a Jewish state.

MAKES NO SENSE!

---

(4) I shall leave you to guess his identity.
(5) The Organization for Education, Science and Culture of the UN.

Where did the idea to turn the Tomb into a mosque and to severe the bond between the Jewish heritage and the Jewish people come from? The idea was adopted after the riots in the Western Wall [6] that broke out in 1996. It was then that the Muslims started to identify the place as the Bilal Aben Rabah mosque.

The first to call it that were the Waqf people [7] in Bethlehem. Later on the name got ingrained in the Palestinian national discourse, and when the conflict about the Israeli fortifications in Rachel's Tomb started, the Palestinian Authority began to refer to the place as a mosque. The unendurable ease of manipulation!

The next stage would be to deny that the Western Wall, the most sacred place for the Jewish people, belongs to the Jews. This, after all, will come sometime. Sounds absurd?

Breaking news! The Palestinians are already making sure to deny the connection between the Western Wall and the Jews.

The Western Wall is one of the four retaining walls that have surrounded the Temple Mount for about two thousand years, since the late Second Temple era until our days. The Second Temple era began with the Return to Zion that marks the return of the Jews from the Babylonian exile to Israel following the Cyrus Cylinder, starting in 538 BC, more than 2500 years before the Ayatollahs in Iran started to deal with denying the Holocaust and with denying the connection between the Jewish people and their homeland.

The Cyrus Cylinder is the declaration by king Cyrus, the founder of the Persian empire, in 538 BC (about 50 years after the destruction of the First Temple), that allows all the nations under his reign to go back and worship their Gods, which included for the people of Israel the return to their land. The ancient Persian leader made sure to restore the exiled Jewish people in their homeland for them to build a Second Temple on the ruins on the First Temple that was destroyed!

The Second Temple was destroyed in 70 AD by Titus, the son of the Emperor Vespasian. Nowadays, a relief, the "Spoils of Jerusalem", depicting the victory parade with the captives from the kingdom of Judea carrying utensils from the temple, hangs on the Arch of Titus in Rome. It is difficult not to notice the seven-branched candelabrum that used to stand in the Jewish Temple.

----

[6] The Western Wall tunnel riots began following the opening of the exit tunnel for tourists. The decision was made by Mr. Benjamin Netanyahu, the Prime Minister of Israel. The Nobel Peace Prize laureate Yasser Arafat urged the "Palestinian people" to react with violence. The riots lasted for 3 days (24 – 27 September 1996).

[7] The "Waqf" is the Muslim administrative body responsible for the Muslim sacred sites.

Over the years the candelabrum has become a symbol of Judaism, and today it is the official symbol of the State of Israel, of many Jewish organizations and of synagogues. The Arch of Titus is an archaeological and historical evidence for the existence of the Jews and the Temple in Jerusalem (unless in the middle of the night, as part of a Zionist conspiracy, the original relief of the destruction of the Palestinian mosque was replaced by a Jewish relief).

The Arch of Titus in Rome: depicts the parade of carrying the spoils of Jerusalem after the Roman conquest in 70 AD.

From Wikipedia under Shutterstock/Matt Ragen

The Palestinian Authority performs a systematic process of changing history and turning Jerusalem into a Palestinian and Muslim territory. In November 2010 a five-page document was published that denies any connection between the holy places and the Jews. The document was written by al-Kotkool Taha, an official at the Palestinian Ministry of Information. The document states that the wall of al-Buraq [8] is the Western

---

[8] This name is used by many Muslims when they talk about the Western Wall. Al-Buraq is a magical beast on which Mohammad rode from Mecca to Al-Aqsa. According to the Muslim tradition Mohammad tied al-Buraq to the Western Wall when he arrived at the Al-Aqsa mosque.

wall of the Al-Aqsa mosque and the Zionist occupation falsely claims ownership of it and names it the Western Wall. [9]

And from talks to actions. On October 10th, 2015, the Palestinians submitted to UNESCO a proposal stating that the Western Wall is an integral part of the Al-Aqsa mosque. The proposal also seeks to acknowledge that the Cave of the Patriarchs [10] and Rachel's Tomb are an integral part of Palestine. As delusional as this may be, there is a very reasonable chance that the resolution will pass due to the automatic majority [11] that the Muslims have in the UN and in its institutions.

An image of Jewish families in the Western Wall in 1880, created by the French artist Alexander Bida. From Wikipedia under "the Western Wall".

---

(9) http://www.nytimes.com/2010/11/26/world/middleeast/26mideast.html , ""Western Wall Feud Heightens Israeli-Palestinian Tensions", By ISABEL KERSHNER, Published: November 25, 2010.

(10) The Cave of the Patriarchs is a building in Eastern Hebron. According to the Jewish tradition and the scriptures, the cave is the burial place of the patriarchs Abraham, Isaac, Jacob and the matriarchs Sarah, Rebecca and Leah. From Wikipedia under "The Cave of the Patriarchs".

(11) The automatic majority is the majority the Muslims have in the UN and its institutions which include 56 Muslim countries and another 100 Non-Aligned countries, a situation that enables to actually pass any resolution, as distorted as it may be while any connection between it and reality is purely coincidental. It is a pity that the UN, that could contribute greatly to world peace, made itself to be irrelevant – more on this in the book I wrote that deals with the total war of the UN against Israel.

If the Palestinian refuse to acknowledge even the relationship of the Jews to Jerusalem, what is the basis on which it is possible to conduct negotiations with people who do not recognize the legitimacy of the State of Israel state in the most sacred places for the Jews?

Not only the Palestinians deny the bond between Israel and Jerusalem and the holy places. The Tourist Office of Israel published an advertisement inviting British people to come and visit Israel. The advertisement includes a photo both of the Western Wall area and the Muslim Dome of the Rock. The British Advertising Association instructed the Israeli Ministry of Tourism to remove the advertisement since these sites are in East Jerusalem, namely, in the "occupied territories." (12)

According to the British Advertising Association the most sacred place to the Jews is not part of Israel, but of the "occupied territories" - whose, the Jordanians? After all, they relinquished the area. On the one hand, it is very difficult to ignore historical evidence regarding the importance of Jerusalem for the Jews. On the other hand, superficiality, incitement and ignorance provide fertile ground for rewriting history with an unendurable ease. The Western Wall was built hundreds of years before the advent of Islam and thousands of years before the showing up of the first Palestinian (sometime in 1964). So how is it possible nevertheless to find a way to explain how a sacred structure to Islam showed up hundreds and thousands of years before the appearance of those who claim it. The solution is presented in the following photo:

```
                        Windows
A fatal exception 0E has occured at E04C:P004bC4h
the current application will be terminated.

* Press any key to terminate the current application.
* Press CTRL+ALT+DELETE again to restart your computer.
  You will lose any unsaved information in all applications.


              Press any key to continue
```

Only an illustration. The actual data are different to those in the photo. _____

(12) http://www.independent.co.uk/news/world/middle-east/israel-tourism-advert-featured-picture-of-occupied-territories-1944066.html

Jerusalem has been the capital of the Jewish people for over 1,600 years before the   first Muslim showed up of on the globe.

Before we delve in the mysteries of history, it is important to know that the mountain where the al-Aqsa mosque and the Dome of the Rock now stand is Mount Moriah. This is the place where Abraham was tested by God in the biblical story the "Binding of Isaac" (13). The First Temple, which was destroyed in 586 B.C. by Nebuchadnezzar the king of Babylon, was built on Mount Moriah. Later, the Second Temple was built and then destroyed by Titus, the son of Vespasian, the Roman Emperor, in 70 A.D. On the ruins of the Temple, the Dome of the Rock was built in 691 A.D.

In 1004 B.C., King David declared Jerusalem as the capital of the Kingdom of Judah. For over 3,000 years the Jews have regarded Jerusalem as their spiritual, political and historical capital, even in times when they did not rule in the city. Throughout history, Jerusalem has been, as it is now, the capital of only one people: the Jews.

King Salomon, the son of David, built the First Temple in Jerusalem. In 586 BC the First Temple was destroyed by the Babylonians, the ancestors of the Iraqi people, who forced the Jews into exile. 50 years later the Jews, who were called then "the people of Israel", were permitted to return following the conquest of Babylon by the Persians, Iran of today. The primary interest of the Jews was to reclaim possession of Jerusalem and rebuild there the Temple called "the Second Temple". Jerusalem has always been more than a political capital for the Kingdom of Judah; it has been also a spiritual center.

During the era of the First Temple and the era of the Second Temple, Jews from all over the Kingdom used to go on pilgrimage to Jerusalem three times a year: On tabernacles, Passover and Pentecost.

The Roman Empire destroyed the Second Temple in 70 AD and put an end to Jewish sovereignty in Jerusalem for nearly two thousand years. The bond with Jerusalem is a powerful spiritual bond for every Jew. During two thousand years of exile the Jews never stopped to think and pray for Jerusalem.

---

(13) The narration of the process of the Binding of Isaac can be found in Wikipedia under "The Binding of Isaac".

Jerusalem is a central element in ceremonies, in prayers, in Jewish holidays and in festivities:

- The Torah Ark, where the Torah scrolls are kept in the synagogues faces, all over the world, toward Jerusalem.
- For over two thousand years the Passover Seder ends with the words "Next year in Jerusalem". These words are uttered also at the end of "Yon Kippur", the most sacred day in the Jewish calendar.
- According to the Jewish religion it is forbidden to get married during three weeks in the summer, to commemorate the breaking through of the walls of Jerusalem by the Babylonian army.

Breaking of the glass ceremony at my wedding

- The "Tisha B'Av fasting" is a Jewish mourning day, commemorating the destruction of the First and the Second temple.
- Jewish wedding ceremonies are mixed with grief over the destruction of Jerusalem. The groom repeats a biblical verse from the Babylonian exile quoted in Psalms chapter KLZ verses E and F: "If I forget thee O Jerusalem may my right hand be forgotten, my tongue stuck to my palate", and then he breaks a glass with his foot to commemorate the destruction of the Temple.

How are the importance and the sanctity attributed to the city by the Muslims expressed?

When Jews pray for Jerusalem they pray toward the Temple Mount. The Muslims pray toward Mecca, so that while in Jerusalem they pray with their backs toward the city. It can be argued that these are merely symbolic matters, but the world is conducted by symbols. Even during a burial, a Muslim's face is turned toward Mecca.

Some of the demands of the Palestinians, regardless of the negotiations, include East Jerusalem as the eternal capital of the historic Palestine. I don't know if you have noticed, but the Palestinians have a few basic demands the Israelis are required to agree to before each negotiation: East Jerusalem as the capital, expulsion of all Jews from the territories of the Palestinian state when it is established, the return of millions of "refugees" to the territory of the State of Israel. From here it is possible to begin to conduct negotiations, when the only question left is: about what?

The covenant of the PLO, the Arab organization that was founded in 1964 and symbolized the early invention of the "Palestinian people", did not mention Jerusalem at all and not its importance to the Muslims and to the Palestinians. Only following the Six Day War in 1967 and the conquest of East Jerusalem from the Jordanians, the covenant was updated to include Jerusalem as well.

Denial of the bond between the Jews and Jerusalem does not stop at only words and statements, but has been going on for decades. The Waqf in Jerusalem is the body responsible for the holy places of the Muslim world. In recent years it has expanded its powers and took over the role of concealing the bond between the Jewish people and Jerusalem and the holy places for the Jews.

After September 2000, the Muslim Waqf closed the Temple Mount site for all archaeological activities carried out by the Israel Antiquities Authority.

The Waqf cleared off 13,000 tons "waste" of Jewish archaeological remains from the times of the First and the Second Temples, some of which were found by Israeli archaeologists in the municipal dump. [14] Thus, by removing the historical evidence, the Waqf turns the whole area into a pure Muslim site.

---

(14) THE DESTRUCTION OF THE TEMPLE MOUNT ANTIQUITIES, http://www.jcpa.org/jl/vp483.ht. Mark Ami-El

Jerusalem City Dump

In June 2007 the "Jerusalem Association of Civil Institutions", an association linked to 130 Palestinian civil institutions, threatened to apply to the UN Secretary General and ask for his support to break away from the municipal authority of the Jerusalem Municipality [15] (The residents of East Jerusalem are considered Israeli citizens and benefit from State services, including National Insurance Services).

According to logic, if they wish to establish their own municipality, they should apply to the Government Authorities in Israel and to authorities such as the Supreme Court or the country's leaders, i.e. the Prime Minister or the President. But since in their statement they do not consider themselves part of the State of Israel, there is some logic in their intention to apply to the UN to get its blessings. It seems like the vision of the Palestinians to see East Jerusalem as their capital, is being realized.

---

(15) http://www.ynet.co.il/articles/0,7340,L-3408086,00.html The Arabs of east Jerusalem to the UN: "We break away", Roy Nahmias.

On the other hand, the Association did not declare its wish to unite with the rest of the Palestinians and with the Palestinian Authority but to be an entity in itself, and the question is: if you are Palestinians, why don`t you unite with your Palestinian brothers in the West Bank [16]?

And if not, who are you actually?

If so, there is only a loose connection between them and their blood brothers in the other parts of the West Bank, just as there is a loose connection between the West Bank and the Gaza Strip.

The real reason is that this is not a nation that has been formed in the course of history. The strongest ties are within the clans and the communities, and less in a "national identity" that takes shape mainly against the "Zionist enemy".

Despite the attempts to deny the ties between the Jewish people and Jerusalem, through endless propaganda or by acts of blurring them committed by the Muslim Waqf, there is no dispute over one thing, over the sources.

The Jews have the bible, the Christians have the New Testament and the Muslims have the Koran. These are the scriptures according to which the customs, the holidays, and the way of life of the believers are derived. These scriptures contain the history of each religion, the activities of the prophets, their doings, their sanctity, the connection they had with God, the promises for salvation and details about the holy places for each religion.

Let us check in these scriptures about Jerusalem. Even the forgers of the elections in Syria, assuming they are still alive, those who always make sure to show how the President of Syrian has been elected time after time with a majority of 99% in the pre- "Arab Spring" era, will find it difficult to falsify these results.

Jerusalem is mentioned in the bible 669 times. In the New Testament Jerusalem is mentioned 154 [17] times. In the Koran:

0

W.N.T.P [18]

(16) As part of erasing the bond between the Jewish people and their historic land the name of the region was changed in the last few decades from Judea and Samaria to the West Bank. How is it possible to name an occupied Palestinian territory after Judah? A pure Jewish name?

(17) http://www.danielpipes.org/84/the-muslim-claim-to-jerusalem

(18) These are the acronyms for What Needs To be Proven. This expression appears often at the end of a mathematical proof or of a philosophical argument.

The preference of the residents of East Jerusalem

We have focused in the book on examining the ties of the Jews to their eternal capital Jerusalem. We have seen how the Palestinians are trying to crumble these ties by various tricks and to create a fake alternative history.

To date, there is a consensus among Israeli citizens, as well, that a peace agreement will include the handing over of East Jerusalem to the Palestinians, for them to establish there their "ancient" capital.

Let us find out what is the opinion of the residents of East Jerusalem on the subject, those proud Palestinians who will in the near future join Palestine and live in their capital (from time immortal).

A survey conducted in November 2010 by the American organization Pechter Middle East Polls that specializes in conducting surveys in the Arab world, exposes the real preferences of the residents of East Jerusalem [19]. The results of the survey are very interesting: even in the case of dividing the city into two capitals, the one of the Israelis and the other of the Palestinians, the "Palestinian" residents of Jerusalem prefer to continue living under the "occupational rule of the Zionist entity".

----

(19) Http://pechter polls.com/?=399, The Palestinians of East Jerusalem: What Do They Really Want? Presentation to the Council on Foreign Relations by Adam Pechter and Dr. David Pollock.

The answers given to the two main questions in the survey leave no room for doubt:

If the solution of "two states to two nations" is successful will you prefer to be a resident of the Palestinian state with all the obligations and the rights or will you prefer to be a resident of the State of Israel?

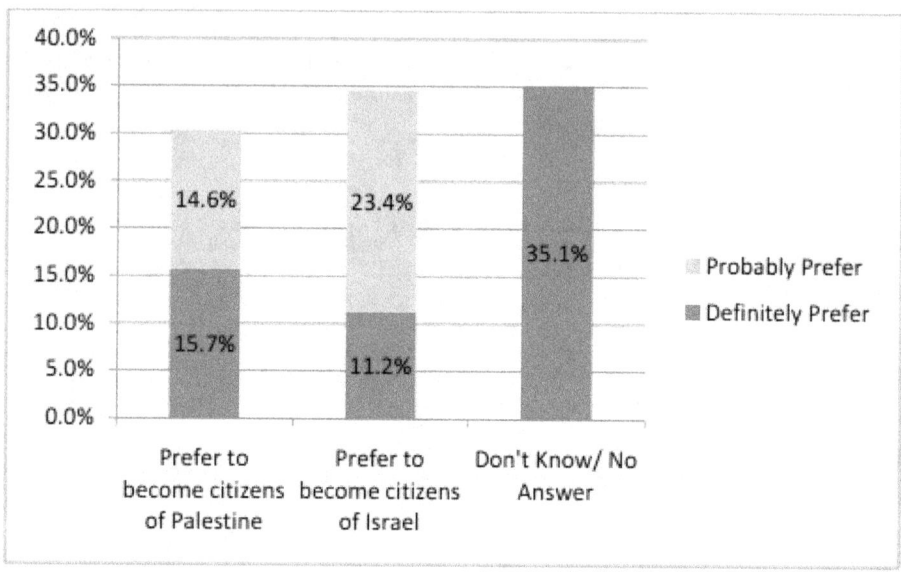

If the solution of "two states to two nations" is successful will the people in your neighborhood prefer to be residents of the Palestinian state with all the obligations and the rights or will they prefer to be residents of the State of Israel?

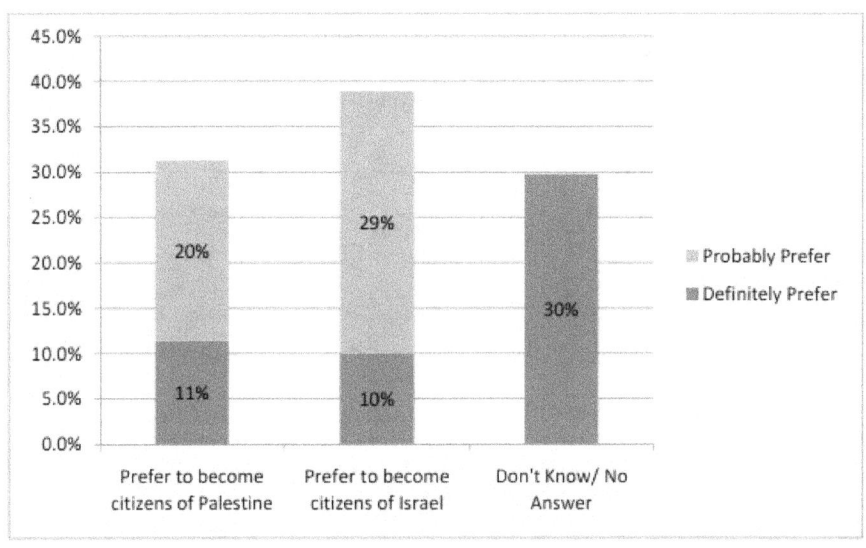

MAKES NO SENSE!

Remember well the results of the survey next time you hear about the collective wish of the Palestinian to establish their historic homeland with Jerusalem as their eternal capital!

To deepen the understanding of the Middle East I encourage you to read attentively the series of books I wrote on this subject.

You can find them under my name: Kobi Shashoua

You are welcome to contact me directly via email:

kobimnsil@gmail.com

And by phone: 972-54-8030648

Website: www.kobisha.com

Yours,

Kobi Shashoua

Every few years Israel is awakened to a brutal bloodbath provoked by the slogan "Al Aqsa is in danger". The latest wave started in October 2015 when this slogan was delivered proudly by clergymen, opinion leaders among the Palestinians and the Arabs living in Israel. This call out was enough to excite many Palestinians and Arabs in Israel to launch an indiscriminate campaign of stabbing and terror among the "Jews". In fact, this call out is unfounded since the status quo regarding the administration of the holy sites in Jerusalem has been uninterrupted for decades, but the facts, in fact, are of no consequence. The wave of terror when every day Jews are stabbed by ecstatic terrorists has become a daily reality in Israel. The religious pretext actually raises the question regarding the status of Jerusalem among religions. Is Jerusalem indeed a religious and national center of the Palestinian people or does it belong to the Jewish people from time immemorial? In this book we shall examine this issue thoroughly and leave the reader to draw the conclusions.

The author, who lives in Israel, the most dangerous neighborhood in the world in the heart of the Middle East, shares with us the facts together with the unique insights and understanding of the region where he lives. We welcome you to participate in this journey from a safe distance.